CHILD CARE LAW

A SUMMARY

ENGLAND AND WALES

Deborah Cullen and Alexandra Conroy Harris

British Association for Adoption & Fostering
(BAAF)
Saffron House
6–10 Kirby Street
London EC1N 8TS
www.baaf.org.uk

Charity registration 275689 (England and Wales) and SCO39337 (Scotland)

© Sixth edition, BAAF, 2014

British Library Cataloguing in Publication Data
A catalogue record for this book is available
from the British Library

ISBN 978 1 910039 22 9

Designed by Helen Joubert Designs
Typeset by Avon DataSet, Bidford on Avon, Warwickshire
Printed in Great Britain by TJ International Ltd, Padstow, Cornwall
Trade distribution by Turnaround Publisher Services, Unit 3, Olympia Trading Estate, Coburg Road,
London N22 6TZ

BAAF is the leading UK-wide membership organisation for all those concerned with adoption,
fostering and child care issues.

Contents

Notes about the authors

Deborah Cullen was the Legal Group Co-ordinator at BAAF until she retired in 2008. *Child Care Law: A summary of the law in England* was first published in 1981. By its second edition in 1986, Deborah Cullen was listed as one of the authors. Deborah was involved in many revised editions of this book until she retired.

Alexandra Conroy Harris was called to the Bar in 1989. She practised as a self-employed barrister in London and the South East, representing local authorities, children and parents in public and private law proceedings. She was employed for nine years as a social services lawyer for a London borough, representing the borough in cases involving children and vulnerable adults and providing training, support and advice to local authority social workers.

Since 2008, she has been employed as the Legal Consultant to BAAF, providing advice to everyone involved in adoption and fostering. She is also the Legal Adviser to the IRM Cymru.

Preface

This booklet is a summary of the main legal provisions for the care of children. For those who do not need to know more, it gives a basic framework. For those starting a more detailed study, it also provides a quick overall view, with references and a bibliography. The content of this book does not constitute legal advice, and does not claim to deal with the difficult questions of law and practice with which this subject abounds, and on which competent legal advice should be sought at an early stage. This booklet does not cover the law in relation to education or criminal offending by children and young persons, nor the detail of requirements for residential establishments for children.

In law a child is a person under 18 – Children Act 1989 section 105(1).

The Children Act 1989 is central to the law concerning the care of children in England and Wales and covers both "private" family law – governing arrangements and disputes between individuals within families – and "public" family law – when local authorities intervene in family life. The adoption of children is governed by the **Adoption and Children Act 2002**. Other relevant statutes are listed below.

There are also numerous statutory instruments (regulations, court rules and orders) determining the detail of applying legislation, and government guidance – mostly to local authorities about good practice in using the law for the benefit of children and their families. The most important of these are summarised in the text.

National Minimum Standards for fostering and adoption services to children provided by local authority and registered private agencies are also referred to in the text.

The law is always subject to change, by amending Acts, Regulations, and case law – the interpretation of legislation by the courts in application to particular cases.

The Westminster Parliament passes the Acts governing England and Wales, but for most aspects of child care law, the power to make regulations has been devolved to the Welsh Assembly.

The first edition of this booklet was written by Diana Rawstron and published in 1980. The second and third editions, published in 1986 and 1992, were revised by Deborah Cullen. Mary Lane and Deborah Cullen revised the fourth and fifth editions, published in 2003 and 2006, and this edition has been updated by Alexandra Conroy Harris.

Summary of main statutes, regulations, rules, guidance and standards

ACTS (IN CHRONOLOGICAL ORDER)

The Children Act 1989

Places the welfare of the child as the paramount concern of the court in making decisions about children in private and public family law matters.

The Act includes legal principles in the "private" care of children within their families, such as the definition of parental responsibility, contains orders providing for the care of children and contact with them when parents separate, and sets out the welfare checklist to be followed by the courts in making decisions about children, when there is a dispute.

The Act also contains orders and principles for the "public" care of children – the responsibilities and duties of local authorities and other public bodies when intervening in family life for children deemed to be at risk, and for supporting children in need and their families.

The Children Act 1989 has been amended by many subsequent statutes, principally by the Children Leaving Care Act 2000, the Care Standards Act 2000, the Adoption and Children Act 2002, the Children Act 2004, the Children and Adoption Act 2006, and the Children and Families Act 2014.

The Human Fertilisation and Embryology Act 1990

Established the Human Fertilisation and Embryology Authority and the law in relation to surrogacy arrangements; licensed clinics providing assisted conception treatments, and the meaning of "parent" when these treatments or arrangements are used. The Act also provides for the making of "parental orders" in surrogacy cases.

The Family Law Act 1996

Amends the Children Act 1989 by providing an order to exclude a person from the child's family home or an area around it, at the time a court makes an emergency protection order or an interim care order. This may avoid the need to remove a child into care by preventing the alleged abuser from coming into contact with the child at home.

The Human Rights Act 1998

This Act gives effect in the UK to rights and freedoms guaranteed under the European Convention on Human Rights. The human rights most relevant to child care law are Article 8 (the right to privacy and family life) and Article 6 (right to a fair trial).

The Adoption (Intercountry Aspects) Act 1999

Provides for regulations to be made about intercountry adoptions under the Hague Convention.

The Carers and Disabled Persons Act 2000

Provides that local authorities can make direct cash payments instead of providing services under section 17 of the Children Act 1989 to a person with parental responsibility for a disabled child or to the young person aged 16 or 17.

The Children (Leaving Care) Act 2000

The Act amends sections 17 and 24 of the Children Act 1989 and imposes new and stronger duties on local authorities to support young people leaving care from 16 years of age until they are at least 18.

The Care Standards Act 2000

The Welsh Assembly and Her Majesty's Chief Inspector of Education, Children's Services and Skills (the CIECSS) are responsible for the registration and inspection of children's homes, voluntary (non-local authority) adoption agencies and independent fostering providers, and the inspection of local authority adoption and fostering services.

The Adoption and Children Act 2002

Is the principal statute governing the placement for and adoption of children in England and Wales. The Act was implemented in full on 30 December 2005 and aligns adoption law with the relevant provisions of the Children Act 1989, to ensure that the welfare of the child is the paramount consideration in all decisions relating to adoption.

This Act also incorporates, with amendments, most of the Adoption (Intercountry Aspects) Act 1999 and amends the Children Act 1989 to introduce special guardianship orders to provide a legal route to permanence for children for whom adoption or a child arrangements order may not be appropriate.

The Children Act 2004

Establishes a Children's Commissioner for England, statutory Local Safeguarding Boards for child protection and, by amendment, Children's Trust Boards. It requires directors of children's services to be appointed by social service authorities and allows for the creation of databases holding information on all children and young people. Section 11 places a duty on key people and bodies to make arrangements to ensure that their functions are discharged with regard to the need to safeguard and promote the welfare of children. It also strengthens the duties of local authorities regarding private fostering. The Act also adds an additional duty for local authorities towards looked after children – to promote their educational achievement.

The Civil Partnership Act 2004 enables same-sex couples to obtain legal recognition of their relationship by registering a civil partnership. The Act amends the Children Act 1989 and the Adoption and Children Act 2002 to provide couples in civil partnerships with the same entitlement to acquire parental responsibility for children as married couples, where one is the birth parent.

The Children and Adoption Act 2006 further amends the law in relation to children by providing the courts with more flexible powers to facilitate contact and enforce orders made under the Children Act 1989.

The Act also provides a statutory framework for the suspension of inter-country adoptions from countries where there are concerns about the process, such as child trafficking.

The Children and Young Persons Act 2008 allows for the establishment of independent social work practices and for the provision of an independent reviewing mechanism in adoption cases. It amends the Children Act 1989 to specify the ways in which local authorities must meet their duties towards accommodated children and to require the use of independent reviewing officers.

The Safeguarding Vulnerable Groups Act 2006 consolidates the lists of people unsuitable to work with children and requires employers to check the suitability of people engaged in regulated activities.

The Human Fertilisation and Embryology Act 2008 amends the HFEA 1990 and extends the class of persons who may be registered as parents of a child to include unmarried and same-sex couples in surrogacy or insemination by donor cases.

The Children, Schools and Families Act 2010 makes provision for the publication of judgements in family proceedings and allows for media access to family courts.

The Children and Families (Wales) Measure 2010 introduces measures to tackle child poverty and to regulate child minding, day care for children and integrated family support teams.

The Protection of Freedoms Act 2012 amends the Safeguarding Vulnerable Groups Act 2006 and amalgamates the Independent Safeguarding Authority with the Criminal Records Bureau to form the Disclosure and Barring Service.

The Children and Families Act 2014 imposes a duty on local authorities to consider fostering to adopt placements, removes the duty to consider the child's religious persuasion, racial origin and cultural and linguistic background when placing for adoption, introduces the use of personal budgets for adoption support and allows the inspection of the Adoption Register by prospective adopters. It amends the Children Act 1989 and the Adoption and Children Act 2002 in respect of contact with regards to children in care and post-adoption and requires care proceedings to be completed within 26 weeks of issue. It applies to England only.

The Social Services and Well-Being (Wales) Act 2014 reforms the law in relation to social services' duties to children and families in Wales. It restates or adapts the local authorities' duties contained in the Children Act 1989.

COURT RULES

The following provide the rules, procedures and prescribed forms for applications to the courts under the Children Act 1989 and Adoption and Children Act 2002.

The Family Procedure Rules 2010 set out the rules and forms for making applications in private and public law applications.

REGULATIONS – LISTED BY TOPIC

1. Placement of children by local authorities in foster, kinship and residential care

The Fostering Services (Wales) Regulations 2003

Govern the approval and review of foster carers by local authorities, voluntary organisations, and independent fostering providers, including the establishment of fostering panels, the duties of agencies with regard to children in foster homes and to foster carers, including foster care and foster placement agreements.

The Placement of Children (Wales) Regulations 2007

Make provision for the arrangements for placement of children by local authorities, voluntary organisations and persons carrying on private children's homes in Wales. The placements may be with foster carers, in community homes, voluntary children's homes or private children's homes and under other arrangements.

The Care Planning, Placement and Case Review (England) Regulations 2010

Set out the obligations of local authorities in planning for and placement of children looked after by them, including children leaving care. Strengthens the role of the independent reviewing officer. Consolidates previous regulations relating to different forms of placements. Introduces temporary approval of connected persons as foster carers.

The Fostering Services (England) Regulations 2011

Make provision about the way in which fostering agencies (independent fostering providers and voluntary organisations) and local authority fostering services are conducted, and in particular about the process for approving foster carers and safeguarding children placed with foster carers.

The Care Planning, Placement and Case Review and Fostering Services (Miscellaneous Amendments) Regulations 2013

Amend the FSR in relation to the approval and change of terms of approval of foster carers and amend the CPPCRR to improve delegation of authority to foster carers. Allow the temporary approval of approved adopters as foster carers for a specific child to support fostering to adopt.

2. Private fostering, day care and child minding

Privately fostered children are children placed with non-related carers by their parents or relatives in private arrangements – these are not children placed with approved carers by local authorities.

The Children (Private Arrangements for Fostering) Regulations 2005 and The Children (Private Arrangements for Fostering) (Wales) Regulations 2006

Require advance notification to the local authority of a private fostering arrangement, and impose duties on local authorities upon receipt of the notification, and visiting private foster homes, speaking to the children, and reporting on the visits.

The Disqualification from Caring for Children (England) Regulations 2002

Set out the categories of persons who are disqualified from privately fostering children unless they first obtain the permission of their local authority. Such people are also prohibited from working in or being involved in the management of children's homes without the consent of the National Care Standards Commission.

The Disqualification from Caring for Children (Wales) Regulations 2004

Make provision for the circumstances in which a person is disqualified from fostering a child privately in Wales.

The Day Care and Child Minding (Disqualification) (England) Regulations 2005 and The Day Care and Child Minding (Disqualification) (England) (Amendment) Regulations 2007

Set out the categories of persons who are disqualified from registration in England as child minders or providers of day care. Persons disqualified under these Regulations may not act as child minders or provide day care. Nor may they be employed in connection with day care provision or directly concerned in the management of any provision of day care.

Day Care and Child Minding (Suitability) (England) Regulations 2005

Set out the information which the Chief Inspector may ask a person applying for registration as a child minder or provider of day care to consent to the disclosure of. Also provide that failure to consent to the disclosure of this information or withdrawal of such consent entitles the Chief Inspector to regard the person as not suitable to look after children under the age of eight or to be in regular contact with such children.

The Child Minding and Day Care Exceptions (Wales) Order 2010

Set out cases where a person will not be considered to be child minding or offering day care for children and so will not fall within the provisions of the Children and Families (Wales) Measure 2010.

3. Complaints and representations by children, relatives and carers

The Children Act 1989 Representations Procedure (England) Regulations 2006 and The Representations Procedure (Wales) Regulations 2014

Set out the procedure to be used by local authorities and voluntary agencies in dealing with complaints and representations about their services to children under the Children Act 1989 and the Adoption and Children Act 2002 – local authorities operate a three-stage complaints procedure.

The Advocacy Services and Representations Procedure (Children) Amendments Regulations 2004 and The Advocacy Services and Representations Procedure (Children) (Wales) Regulations 2004

Impose a duty on local authorities to provide advocacy services for children wishing to make complaints under the Children Act 1989 representations procedure. Section 26A requires local authorities to make arrangements for the provision of assistance including, by way of representation, to care leavers and children who make or intend to make representations or complaints under sections 24D and 26(3) of the Children Act 1989.

4. Reviews of children looked after by local authorities

The Care Planning, Placement and Case Review (England) Regulations 2010 and The Review of Children's Cases (Wales) Regulations 2007

Govern the way in which local authorities and voluntary organisations review cases of children they are looking after, including the timing of reviews. They impose obligations on the "responsible authority" (a local authority or voluntary organisation looking after the child or a person carrying on a private children's home) to appoint an Independent Reviewing Officer (IRO) in connection with the review of each case of a child looked after or for whom accommodation is being provided. They also require the local authority to inform the IRO about any significant change of circumstances following a review or a significant failure to implement decisions made as a result of a review.

The Adoption Agencies Regulations 2005 and **Adoption Agencies (Wales) Regulations**

Govern the frequency and content of reviews of children authorised to be placed for adoption and placed with adoptive families.

5. Secure accommodation

The Children (Secure Accommodation) Regulations 1991

Set out the procedure to be followed by local authorities in consider-ing placing children in secure accommodation and applying for orders authorising secure placement under section 25 of the Children Act 1989.

The Children Secure Accommodation (No 2) Regulations 1991

The Children (Secure Accommodation) Amendment Regulations 1995

The Children (Secure Accommodation) (Amendment) (England) Regulations 2012

The Children (Secure Accommodation) (Amendment) (Wales) Regulations 2013

These Regulations amend the Children (Secure Accommodation) Regulations 1991 in connection with the extension of provision of secure accommodation.

6. Children leaving care or ceasing to be looked after

Children (Leaving Care) (England) Regulations 2001 and Children (Leaving Care) (Wales) Regulations 2001

Make provision for support for children and young people aged 16 and over who are or have been looked after by a local authority.

7. Regulation of care homes for children

The Children's Homes Regulations 2001 and **The Children's Homes (Wales) Regulations 2002**

Govern the conduct, suitability, staffing and management of children's homes in England and Wales to ensure compliance with the National Minimum Standards for Children's Homes.

The Children's Homes (Wales) (Miscellaneous Amendments) Regulations 2007, The Children's Homes (Amendment) Regulations 2011 and The Children's Homes and Looked after Children (Miscellaneous Amendments) (England) Regulations 2013

These regulations amend the original regulations in respect of the conduct of children's homes.

8. Adoption

Adoption Agencies Regulations 2005 and Adoption Agencies (Wales) Regulations 2005

Govern the way in which adoption agencies and their adoption panels are required to carry out their functions under the Adoption and Children Act 2002, including preparation and approval of prospective adopters, consideration of whether children should be placed for adoption, matching prospective adopters with children and supervision and review of adoptive placements.

The Restriction on the Preparation of Adoption Reports Regulations 2005

These regulations apply to England and Wales, and place restrictions on the persons who may prepare reports about the suitability of a child for adoption, the suitability of a person to adopt a child, or about the adoption or placement for adoption of a child, in both domestic and intercountry adoptions.

The Suitability of Adopters Regulations 2005

Apply in respect of adoption agencies in England only, and prescribe the matters to be taken into account by an adoption agency in determining, or making any report in respect of, the suitability of any person to adopt a child, and require the adoption agency, in determining the suitability of a prospective adoptive couple, to have proper regard to the need for stability and permanence in their relationship.

The Welsh equivalent of these regulations is contained within the **Adoption Agencies (Wales) Regulations 2005.**

The Adoption and Children (Miscellaneous Amendments) Regulations 2005, The Local Authority (Adoption) (Miscellaneous Provisions) Regulations 2005, The Voluntary Adoption Agencies (Amendment) Regulations 2005, The Local Authority Adoption Service (England) (Amendment) Regulations 2005, The Independent Review of Determinations (Adoption) Regulations 2005, The Voluntary Adoption Agencies and the Adoption Agencies (Miscellaneous Amendments) (Amendment) Regulations 2009, The Adoption Agencies and Independent Review of Determinations (Amendment) Regulations 2011, The Adoption Agencies (Panel and Consequential Amendments) Regulations 2012, The Adoption Agencies (Miscellaneous Amendments) Regulations 2013, and **The Adoption and Care Planning (Miscellaneous Amendments) Regulations 2014**

These regulations amend the Adoption Agencies Regulations 2005 in respect of adoption agencies in England.

The Independent Review of Determinations (Adoption) (Wales) Regulations 2005, The Local Authority (Non-agency Adoptions) (Wales) Regulations 2005, The Local Authority Adoption Service (Wales) Regulations 2005, The Independent Review of Determinations (Adoption) (Wales) Regulations 2006, The Local Authority Adoption Service (Wales) Regulations 2007, The Independent Review of Determinations (Adoption and Fostering) (Wales) Regulations 2010, The Adoption Agencies (Wales) (Amendment) Regulations 2012 and The Adoption Agencies (Wales) (Amendment) Regulations 2014

These regulations amend the Adoption Agencies (Wales) Regulations 2005 in respect of adoption agencies in Wales.

9. Access to information about adoptions

The Disclosure of Adoption Information (Post-Commencement Adoptions) Regulations 2005 and The Access to Information (Post-Commencement Adoptions) (Wales) Regulations 2005

Govern how adoption agencies keep information about each adoption and deal with applications for disclosure of such information. The regime applies in relation to persons adopted on or after 30 December 2005.

The Adoption Information and Intermediary Services (Pre-Commencement Adoptions) Regulations 2005 and The Adoption Information and Intermediary Services (Pre-Commencement) Adoption (Wales) Regulations 2005

Make provision under section 98 of the Adoption and Children Act 2002 for the purposes of assisting persons adopted before 30 December 2005 to obtain information about their adoption and to facilitate contact between those persons and their birth relatives.

13

The Adopted Children and Adoption Contact Registers Regulations 2005

Apply in England and Wales and govern the Adopted Children Register and the Adoption Contact Register maintained by the Registrar General, including the obtaining of information from the register and the connection between this register and birth records.

10. Adoption support

The Adoption Support Services Regulations 2005 – for England and **The Adoption Support Services (Local Authorities) (Wales) Regulations 2005**

Make provision for local authorities to provide adoption support services as part of the service maintained by them under the Adoption and Children Act 2002.

11. Intercountry adoption

The Adoptions with a Foreign Element Regulations 2005

Apply to England and Wales and make provision relating to intercountry adoptions under the Adoption (Intercountry Aspects) Act 1999 and the Adoption and Children Act 2002, and Part 3 provides for adoptions under the 1993 Hague Convention on Protection of Children and Co-operation in respect of Intercountry Adoption.

12. Special guardianship

The Special Guardianship Regulations 2005 and The Special Guardianship (Wales) Regulations 2005

Govern special guardianship orders provided for in sections 14A–14C Children Act 1989, and special guardianship support services.

Summary of main statutes, regulations, rules, guidance and standards

GUIDANCE

The Government publishes guidance to local authorities and voluntary agencies setting out the detail of how statutes, regulations and court rules are to be applied in their work with children and families.

Statutory Guidance is issued under section 7 of the Local Authorities and Social Services Act 1970. As such, it does not have the full force of law, but must be complied with by local authorities unless circumstances indicate exceptional reasons to justify a variation.

CHILD CARE AND CHILD PROTECTION

The main statutory guidance in relation to the Children Act 1989, regulations and court rules is contained in nine volumes published by the Department of Health in 1991 and periodically updated by the Department for Education. Now available online only.

The Framework for the Assessment of Children in Need and their Families
(Department of Health, 2000 and National Assembly for Wales, 2001)
Outlines a framework for use by all those who work with children and families determining whether a child is in need under the Children Act 1989 and deciding how best to provide help.

Working Together to Safeguard Children (HM Government) and
Safeguarding Children: Working Together under the Children Act 2004 (Welsh Assembly Government 2007)

Sets out the key arrangements for safeguarding and promoting the welfare of children. It applies to all those key local people and bodies named under section 11(1) of the Children Act 2004. Part 1 of the guidance sets out the arrangements that are likely to be common to all or most of the agencies to which the duty applies. Part 2 deals with implementation in each particular agency to which the section 11 duty applies. The guidance lists references to a number of other government publications relevant to child protection.

Independent Reviewing Officers Handbook

Published in 2010 and provides guidance as to the role and functions of Independent Reviewing Officers for looked after children.

Statutory Guidance on Adoption (Department for Education, 2014)

Covers the legislative requirements and expectations on local authorities and voluntary adoption agencies in arranging adoptions for children for whom adoption is the best permanence outcome for them, including intercountry adoptions. It also covers the legislative requirements on adoption agencies and adoption support agencies in the disclosure of information and facilitating contact for adopted adults and birth families.

The Adoption Agencies (Wales) Regulations 2005 Guidance (National Assembly for Wales, 2006)

Gives statutory guidance to Welsh adoption agencies.

Special Guardianship Guidance

Provides statutory guidance for local authorities in England to the special guardianship provisions in the Children Act 1989 and the Regulations including support services.

Guidance in National Standards

Under the Care Standards Act 2000, the Government has published:

*   National Minimum Standards for Children's Homes
*   National Minimum Standards for Adoption

- National Minimum Standards for Fostering Services

- National Minimum Standards for Private Fostering

Compliance with Minimum Standards is a significant measure against which local authorities, adoption agencies and children's homes are registered and inspected.

ABBREVIATIONS

AAR 2005 means the Adoption Agencies Regulations 2005

ACA 2002 means the Adoption and Children Act 2002

AFER 2005 means the Adoptions with a Foreign Element Regulations 2005

ASR 2005 means the Adoption Support Services Regulations 2005

CA 1989 means the Children Act 1989

CFA 2014 means the Children and Families Act 2014

CSA 2000 means the Care Standards Act 2000

CPA 2004 means the Civil Partnership Act 2004

CPPCR 2010 means the Care Planning, Placement and Case Review Regulations 2010

FSR 2011 means the Fostering Services (England) Regulations 2011

FPR 2010 means the Family Procedure Rules 2010

HFEA 1998 means the Human Fertilisation and Embryology Act 1998

Review Regs means the CPPCR 2010 and Review of Children's Cases (Wales) Regulations 2007

SAR 2005 means the Suitability of Adopters Regulations 2005

SGR 2005 means the Special Guardianship Regulations 2005

Terms used

Parental responsibility is defined by the Children Act 1989 as 'all the rights, duties, powers and responsibilities which by law a parent has in relation to a child and his property'.

This includes the legal entitlement to make decisions about a child – name, education, place of residence, medical treatment, etc, and, for birth parents, guardians and special guardians only, consent to placement for adoption, and to the making of adoption orders.

CAFCASS – The Children and Family Court Advisory and Support Service is a national public body for England set up to safeguard and promote the welfare of children involved in family court proceedings. It is accountable to Parliament through the Department for Education (DfE). CAFCASS is independent of the courts, social services, education and health authorities and all similar agencies.

In Wales this service, on similar terms to CAFCASS, is governed by the Welsh Assembly – with Welsh Family Proceedings Officers (WFPOs).

Parental responsibility and private family life

A1 Which birth parents have parental responsibility?

When a child is born to married parents, both have parental responsibility from birth.

If the parents are unmarried, and the child's birth was registered before 1 December 2003, the mother alone has parental responsibility from birth.

If the child's birth was jointly registered by the mother and unmarried birth father on or after 1 December 2003, the birth father shares parental responsibility equally with the birth mother.

CA 1989 section 4A(1) and ACA 2002 section 111(2)(a)

The unmarried birth father may also acquire parental responsibility by formal agreement with the mother or by a parental responsibility order, by marrying the mother after the child's birth, or by an adoption order granted to the unmarried father, in special circumstances.

CA 1989 sections 2 and 4 and ACA 2002 section 51(4)

A2 Birth fathers without parental responsibility

A birth father without parental responsibility is a legal parent under the Children Act 1989 in the sense that he must be notified of legal proceedings concerning his children, be involved in any local authority decision-making about them, including attendance at meetings, and is entitled to contact with his children after separation from the children's mother or the children becoming looked after by the local authority, unless court orders to the contrary are made.

However, when a birth father does not have parental responsibility, he is not entitled to make decisions about his children, such as a change of name, education, place of residence, medical treatment, etc, unless the child's mother or other persons with parental responsibility agree, or section 8 Children Act 1989 orders are made.

Birth fathers and adoption – see Section H

A3 Guardians and parental responsibility

A guardian (not a special guardian) is a person who has been appointed to act in the place of a parent after the parent's death. The appointment may be made in writing by a parent or an existing guardian or the court.

CA 1989 section 5(1)–(4)

Where the parents of a child both have parental responsibility, they both have the power to appoint a guardian to act after their deaths. While one parent is still alive, any guardian appointed by the other will usually only assume parental responsibility after the death of the surviving parent. If, however, there was a child arrangements order specifying that the child should live with the parent who has died, then that parent's appointment of the guardian takes effect immediately on the appointer's death.

Where a child's parents were not married to each other, only the mother has the power to appoint a guardian, unless the father has acquired parental responsibility.

A court may appoint a guardian for a child who has no parent with parental responsibility for him or her, or following the death of a parent or guardian who had a residence order in his or her favour at the time of death.

A guardian may also appoint one or more individuals to be guardian(s) after his or her death.

A guardian has parental responsibility for the child, including the right to consent or withhold consent to placement for adoption, or adoption.

Guardianship continues until the child reaches the age of 18 unless terminated earlier by court order or by the death of the guardian.

A4 Special guardians and parental responsibility

See Section B7.

A5 Relatives and parental responsibility

In the Children Act 1989, a relative is a child's grandparent, brother, sister, uncle or aunt (by full or half blood), or by marriage or civil partnership, or a step-parent.

CA 1989 section 105(1) amended by CPA 2004 section 75(4)

In the Adoption and Children Act 2002, a relative means grandparent, brother, sister, uncle or aunt by full or half blood, or by marriage or civil partnership. This does not include a great aunt or uncle or great grandparent.

In section 1 ACA 2002, "relative" includes the mother and father of the child (whether or not the father has parental responsibility).

ACA 2002 section 144 amended by section 29(11) of CPA 2004

Relatives of a child have some entitlement under CA 1989 to apply for section 8 orders and special guardianship orders, and under ACA 2002 to adopt children within the family.

A6 Step-parents and parental responsibility

A step-parent *who is married to or the civil partner of* the birth parent of a child can acquire parental responsibility by:

- **agreement with each of the birth parents with parental responsibility** – parental responsibility is shared with each of these parents.

- **the granting of a parental responsibility order** – parental responsibility is shared with each parent with parental responsibility.

CA 1989 section 4A(1)(b)

A7 Other individuals and parental responsibility

Individuals other than parents can acquire parental responsibility by:

- **adoption order**, in which case the adoptive parents acquire all the responsibility formerly held by the parents and that of the parents and others is extinguished (see Section H).

ACA 2002 section 46(2)(a)

- **being appointed guardians** after a parent's death – giving guardians all the parental responsibility that parents would have (see Section A3).

CA 1989 section 5

- **the making of a child arrangements order** – where a court makes an order specifying that a child should live with a person, that person shares parental responsibility with the birth parents and any others with parental responsibility.

CA 1989 section 12

- **the granting of a parental order** – full and permanent parental responsibility is conveyed by this order to a married couple for a child born in surrogacy, where at least one of the couple is a genetic parent of the child. The birth mother's parental responsibility is extinguished (see Section A9).

HFEA 2008 section 54

- **placement order** – a local authority placing a child for adoption shares parental responsibility with the prospective adopter.

ACA 2002 section 25(4)

- **the granting of a special guardianship order** – the special guardians share parental responsibility with the birth parents with parental responsibility, and can exercise it to the exclusion of birth parents on most but not all issues (see Section B7).

CA 1989 section 14 A–F

- **a second female parent** – a woman who is the partner of, but not married to or the civil partner of, a child's mother, will be a 'second female parent' if she is part of the fertility treatment of the child's mother and fulfils the required formalities (HFEA 2008 section 43). She can acquire parental responsibility by being registered on the child's birth certificate, entering into a parental responsibility agreement or the court making a parental responsibility order.

CA 1989 section 42A

A8 Parental responsibility and local authorities

Local authorities can acquire parental responsibility for children by:

- **the granting of an emergency protection order** which gives the local authority temporary and limited parental responsibility.

CA 1989 section 44

- **the granting of a care order including an interim care order** whereby the local authority acquires parental responsibility which is shared with the parents, and any guardians or special guardians. The local authority is entitled to decide the extent to which parents, guardians or special guardians can exercise their parental responsibility, and has the right to decide where and with whom a child lives.

CA 1989 section 33(3)

- **the granting of a placement order or formal parental consent to a child's placement for adoption.** The local authority acquires parental responsibility for the child – shared with the birth parents or others with parental responsibility, and with the prospective adopters upon placement.

ACA 2002 sections 21 and 25(1) (2) and (3) and sections 19 and 25(1) and (2)

A9 Parental responsibility and assisted conception or surrogacy

Mothers

The gestational mother of a child born as a result of assisted conception or by surrogacy is treated in law as the legal mother of the child and has parental responsibility from birth.

HFEA 2008 section 33

Fathers

Where the sperm used in assisted conception is that of the mother's partner, he will be the father of the child – with parental responsibility if married to the mother, and without it if not.

Where conception is achieved using the sperm of a donor and not that of the mother's partner, paternity will depend in law on whether the mother's partner consented to the treatment at the time the treatment was carried out.

The partner – unless it is shown that he did not consent to the treatment, or did not consent at the time it was carried out – will be treated in law as the father of the child. If he is married to the mother, he will have parental responsibility; if he is not, he will only be able to acquire parental responsibility by agreement with the mother, by court order or by registering the birth (see A2).

HFEA 2008 section 35
Re R (IVF: Paternity of Child) (2005) UKHL 33

Where conception is achieved by anonymous sperm donation via a registered clinic, and the mother has no partner or husband who consented to the treatment, or the child is conceived from sperm donation after the donor's death, the child has no legal father.

HFEA 2008 section 41

Second female parent

Where a woman is married to or the civil partner of the mother of a child conceived through assisted conception, she will be treated as the parent of the child unless she did not consent to the treatment. If she is not married to or the civil partner of the mother, and the assisted conception takes place in a licensed clinic, she will be treated as a parent of the child if she has met the agreed female parenthood conditions at the time of treatment. These require that both the mother and the proposed female parent consent in writing to the treatment and parenthood.

HFEA 2008 sections 42, 43 and 44

Human Fertilisation and Embryology (Deceased Fathers) Act 2003

Makes provision about the circumstances in which, and the extent to which, a man is to be treated in law as the father of a child where the child has resulted from certain fertility treatment undertaken after the man's death.

Surrogacy

Where a child is born to a surrogate mother, her husband (if he consented to the surrogacy) is the father of the child in law, and has parental responsibility. If he did not consent, he is not treated in law as the father (the genetic father is then a father without parental responsibility).

If she is not married, the surrogate mother alone has parental responsibility.

HFEA 1990 section 28

The commissioning parents

The people who commission surrogacy (and usually provide the sperm and/or ovum) are not in law the parents of the child, and have no parental responsibility until and unless they acquire it by the making of a parental order, or they adopt the child, or, in the case of the commissioning father, he is able to acquire it by making a parental responsibility agreement with the gestational mother or jointly registering the child's birth.

HFEA 1990 section 30

A10 Children's rights and parental responsibility

The rights which parents and others with parental responsibility exercise on behalf of their children, such as consent to medical treatment and contraception, diminish as children increase in age and maturity. This is recognised in provisions of the Children Act 1989 and the Adoption and Children Act 2002, for example, allowing children of sufficient under-standing to make their own applications to courts, and to refuse medical and psychiatric examination.

However, a young person's refusal to consent can still be overruled by those with parental responsibility or a court.

Private arrangements for the care of children

B1 Caring for children at home

There are no explicit statutory controls over arrangements parents make to have their children looked after in their own homes, whether this care is provided by a relative, friend, nanny, au pair or anyone else. However, if parents leave a child with a carer whom they have not assured themselves is suitable, or who is known to them not to be suitable, and who abuses the child, the harm to the child may be deemed as attributable to the care given by the parents – one of the grounds for a care order or supervision order (see Section D).

B2 Children at home alone

It is not in itself an offence to leave children unattended, although if children are being neglected the local authority may intervene to protect them or even to remove them (see Section D) and certain conduct may render a parent, a babysitter or any caregiver liable to criminal prosecution. For example, an offence of cruelty to children (which can include neglect or abandonment) and another of exposing children under the age of 12 to risk of burning.

B3 Day care provision outside the home

There are five categories of day care provision.

B3.1 Early Years Foundation Stage Framework

The Early Years Foundation Stage (EYFS) in England sets standards for the learning, development and care of children from birth to five years old. All schools and Ofsted-registered early years providers must follow the EYFS, including child minders, preschools, nurseries and school reception classes.

Statutory framework for the Early Years Foundation Stage, Department for Education, 2014

National Minimum Standards for Regulated Child Care

In Wales, the Welsh Government produces a set of 24 minimum standards that all child care providers are expected to meet.

National Minimum Standards for Regulated Child Care, Welsh Government, 2012

Day care provision, which does not meet these standards, will not be registered, or if found to be not complying on inspection, will have its registration cancelled. Failure to pay the annual fee for registration and inspection will also risk cancellation of registration.

CA 1989 Part XA and CSA 2000 Part VI for Wales
CSA 2000 Part VI and Child Care Act 2006 for England

B3.2 Inspection and regulation of day care

In England, all day care providers must be registered and inspected by Her Majesty's Inspector of Schools through Ofsted. Guidance is available from www.ofsted.gov.uk.

In Wales, the Welsh Assembly is responsible for registration and inspection of day care provision through the Care and Social Services Inspectorate Wales (CSSIW). Guidance is available from www.cssiw.org.uk.

B3.3 Full day care

Facilities that provide day care for children aged under eight for a period of four hours or more in any day in non-domestic premises, e.g. day nurseries and children's centres and some family centres.

B3.4 Child minding

In England, child minding is defined as the provision of childcare on domestic premises for reward.

Child Care Act 2006 section 96(4)

In Wales, a childminder is someone who looks after one or more children under the age of eight in domestic premises (other than the home of the person employing the childminder) for reward for more than two hours a day or for a longer period of up to 28 days and is not a relative or a person who has parental responsibility for the child.

CA 1989 section 79

B3.5 Crèches

Facilities providing occasional care for children under eight in particular premises for more than five days a year. Registration is required where crèches open for more than two hours a day.

B3.6 Out of school care

Day care for children under eight and in use before or after school and/or during school holidays, for more than two hours a day and for more than five days a year.

B3.7 Sessional care

Children under eight are looked after for a session that is less than four hours in any day in non-domestic premises, e.g. playgroups.

Where two or more sessions are offered in any one day, children must not attend more than five sessions a week and there must be a break of at least one hour between sessions with no children in the care of the provider.

B4 Private fostering

A privately fostered child is someone

● who is under 16 (or under 18 if with disabilities)

● who is cared for and living in accommodation provided by someone who is not a parent, relative, person with parental responsibility for him or her or an approved local authority foster carer, for 28 days or more, whether or not there is any payment.

If a child is looked after by a non-relative for up to 27 days, he or she does not become a foster child unless it is intended that the fostering will continue beyond that period. Thus casual arrangements, such as friends looking after a child while the parents take a holiday, do not create a fostering relationship.

CA 1989 section 66

A child is not privately fostered if he or she has been placed for adoption by an adoption agency or the local authority has duties to monitor the welfare of the child under adoption legislation.

CA 1989 Schedule 8 para 5

B4.1 Notification to the local authority

A private foster carer must notify the local authority children's services department at least six weeks before a child is placed, or immediately if the child is received in an emergency. Regulations specify the information to be included in the notification, and the action to be taken by the local authority upon receipt of the notification, and the requirement for parents and the private foster carers to notify of the commencement and end of the private fostering arrangements.

The Children (Private Arrangements for Fostering) Regulations 2005 English and Welsh Regs 3–6, and 9 and 10

B4.2 Welfare of privately fostered children

The local authority has a duty to be satisfied that the welfare of all privately fostered children in its area is being safeguarded.

CA 1989 section 67

Regulations set out the duties of the local authority to visit private foster homes, speak to the children, report on the visits, and speak to every parent with parental responsibility where practicable.

The Children (Private Arrangements for Fostering) Regulations 2005 Regs 7–12 and schedule 3

The local authority may prohibit private fostering or impose conditions such as the number, age and sex of the children, medical facilities or fire precautions.

CA 1989 section 69
Disqualification from Caring for Children (England) Regulations 2002

Private foster carers do not have parental responsibility for their foster children and must usually return them to their parents, or others with parental responsibility, on request. Parents may, however, delegate certain functions to foster carers, such as the right to authorise medical treatment.

Private foster carers can apply for a residence order if they have the consent of each parent or person who has parental responsibility for the child, or the child has lived with them for a period of at least three years, or they have the court's leave.

CA 1989 sections 8 and 9, and 10(5) (b) and (c)(iii)

B5 Voluntary organisations

Children may be accommodated by a voluntary society such as Barnardo's, the Church of England Children's Society or the NCH Action for Children. These organisations are guided by the terms of their own foundations and are subject to statutory regulation. Children accommodated by them may be looked after in a residential home, fostered or, if the society is also a registered adoption agency, placed for adoption. Many of the duties placed on local authorities looking after children apply also to voluntary organisations.

CA 1989 Part VII and Schedule 5, and Fostering and Adoption Standards and Regulations

Arrangements under Part VII of the Children Act 1989 are to be distinguished from those where local authorities use the services of a voluntary or independent agency to provide care for children they are looking after (see E4.3).

Local authorities have a duty to satisfy themselves that voluntary organisations accommodating children within their area are promoting the children's welfare, and must arrange for the children to be visited from time to time.

CA 1989 section 62

B6 Orders under the Children Act 1989

B6.1 Principles to be applied by the court

When a court makes any decision about a child's upbringing or the administration of a child's property, the child's welfare is the court's paramount consideration.

CA 1989 section 1(1)

The court is also required to have regard to the general principle that delay in determining any question about a child's upbringing is likely to prejudice the child's welfare.

The Children Act 1989 sets out a checklist of factors to which courts must have regard in determining disputed cases under the Act. These apply to applications for section 8 orders and applications for care or supervision orders or for contact with a child in care, and special guardianship orders.

CA 1989 section 1(3) and (4)

A court must not make any order under the Children Act unless it considers that it would be better for the child than making no order.

CA 1989 section 1(5)

Courts considering applications for section 8 or special guardianship orders may appoint an officer from CAFCASS (the Children and Family Court Advisory and Support Service) or a Welsh Family Proceedings Officer (WFPO) to assist in deciding what order, if any, is in a child's best interests.

B6.2 Section 8 orders

There are three orders that a court may make under section 8 – **child arrangements, specific issues** and **prohibited steps**. These orders are available principally to parents who cannot agree about their exercise of parental responsibility, as well as to fathers without parental responsibility, and in some circumstances they are also available to other family members or people with an interest in the child, e.g. foster carers.

CA 1989 sections 8–10

B6.3 Child arrangements orders

A child arrangements order is an order settling with whom a child should live and when and how they should spend time or have contact with any person. When a child arrangements order says that a child should live with a person who does not otherwise have parental responsibility, that person will have parental responsibility for as long as the order is in force, but will not have the right to consent or withhold consent to the child's placement for adoption, or to the making of an adoption order, or to the appointment of a guardian for the child unless he is the child's birth father.

B6.4

As well as parents, certain other people are entitled to apply for child arrangements orders. These include anyone applying with the agreement of all the people who have parental responsibility and anyone with whom the child has lived for three years in the recent past, or local authority foster carers after one year (see below). In addition, anyone, including the child, may ask the court for permission to apply for any section 8 order. Local authorities may not apply for child arrangements orders.

CA 1989 sections 9 and 10 as amended by ACA 2002 section 114 and CFA 2014 section 12

B6.5

An application for a child arrangements order settling with whom a child should live may be made for a child subject to a care order, and that order discharges the care order. Local authority foster carers can apply for child arrangements orders for looked after children in their care without the permission of the local authority if the child has lived with them for the previous 12 months.

CA 1989 section 91(a) as amended

B6.6

A child arrangements order comes to an end when a child reaches 16, unless the court specifies that it is to last up to the child's 18th birthday, which it may do only if there are exceptional circumstances.

This does not apply to child arrangements orders specifying with whom a child should live.

CA 1989 sections 9 and 12 as amended

B6.7

While a child arrangements order settling with whom a child should live is in force, a local authority may, but is not legally obliged to, pay an allowance towards the cost of the child's maintenance, as long as the child is not living with a parent or step-parent.

CA 1989 Schedule 1 paragraph 15

B6.8

A **child arrangements order (section 8)** can require the person with whom the child lives to allow the child to have contact with the person(s) named in the order. Contact can include letters, cards, or other forms of correspondence (indirect contact), as well as, or instead of, face-to-face or direct contact. Courts can specify the exact arrangements for contact, e.g. whether it is supervised or not. Contact orders are usually made where a child's parents cannot agree about contact arrangements after their separation. However, they are also relevant to contact for a child who is the subject of a special guardianship order (see Section H for contact and adoption).

CA 1989 sections 8 and 11(7)

B6.9

Specific issue orders – the court determines any question in connection with the exercise of parental responsibility for a child (except with whom a child should live or spend time), e.g. decisions about medical treatment or education.

B6.10

Prohibited steps orders ban a person from taking a particular step in the exercise of parental responsibility (e.g. preventing a parent from allowing the child to associate with a particular person, or emigration).

None of the above orders, except a child arrangements order dealing with living arrangements, may be made when a child is subject to a care order or interim care order. There are also restrictions on making such orders where the child is awaiting adoption – see Section H.

B7 Special guardianship orders

This order is a "halfway house" between a child arrangements order and an adoption order. The order gives parental responsibility to the special guardians, shared with the birth parents, but allows the special guardians to exercise parental responsibility to the exclusion of birth parents on most issues (except adoption). The special guardianship order comes to an end when the child is 18 years of age.

CA 1989 section 14A, as introduced by the ACA 2002 section 113

The special guardian cannot cause the child to be known by a new surname or removed from the UK for more than three months without the leave of court, or written permission of each parent with parental responsibility.

Unlike adoption, the legal identity of the child does not change – they remain the child of their birth parents – and their nationality does not change. The birth parents remain liable for child support.

The special guardianship order is intended to be more permanent and more secure than a child arrangements order.

Birth parents need the leave of court to apply to discharge a special guardianship order.

A special guardianship order discharges a care order, but is not discharged by the granting of a care order.

CA 1989 section 14A–14C

B7.1 Who may apply for special guardianship orders

Applicants must be at least 18. Two or more individuals may be made joint special guardians.

Birth parents cannot apply.

Special guardianship is not intended as an alternative to step-parent adoption since the making of a special guardianship order to a step-parent would enable him or her to exercise parental responsibility to the exclusion of their partner – the birth parent.

CA 1989 section 14A(2) and (3) and section 10(9)

Those who can apply as of right for a special guardianship order (and do not need leave of the court) include the child's guardians, people named as the person with whom a child should live under a child arrangements order, those with whom a child has lived for three years or more during the preceding five years, and those with consent of parents and others with parental responsibility, including the consent of a local authority with parental responsibility for the child.

LA foster carers can apply within one year of placement with the permission of the local authority that has parental responsibility for the child, and after one year of placement without that permission.

CA 1989 section 14A(5) and (3)

Others (e.g. relatives) can apply with permission of the court.

CA 1989 section 9(3)

B7.2 Notice to the local authority

Applicants for special guardianship orders must give written notice to the local authority (where they live, or the local authority looking after the child) of their intention to apply for the order, at least three months before making the application.

CA 1989 section 14A(7)

B7.3 Local authority investigation and court report

On receipt of the notice, the local authority must investigate and prepare a report for the court.

CA 1989 section 14A(8)

A court cannot make a special guardianship order until it has received a report by the local authority about the suitability of the applicants.

CA 1989 section 14A(11)

B7.4 Special guardianship orders made on the court's own initiative

A court can make a special guardianship order with respect to a child in any family proceedings even though no application has been made (after receiving the local authority's report).

CA 1989 section 14A(6) (b) and (11)

B7.5 Special guardianship support services

A local authority has a duty to provide support services generally to special guardianship families (financial and other support) and the discretion to provide support services to individual special guardianship families.

Local authorities have a duty to assess special guardianship families for support services on request *if the child is looked after by the local authority or*

was looked after immediately before the special guardianship order was made.
SG Regulations 2005 Regs 3–20

B7.6 Leaving care provisions and special guardianship

Children who were looked after by a local authority before the making of a special guardianship order may qualify for advice and assistance under the Children Act 1989 and the Children (Leaving Care) Act 2000, if they:

(a) are 16 to 20 years old, or if less than 18, have an SGO in force, or

(b) if 18 or above, had an SGO in force when they reached that age, and were looked after by a local authority immediately before the making of an SGO.

CA 1989 Section 24(1A)
SG Regulations 2005

B8 Wardship and the inherent jurisdiction of the High Court

Wardship is a means by which the inherent jurisdiction of the High Court may be exercised with regard to children. It is a power that does not come from statute, although the Children Act 1989 places limits on the way it may be used, and other statutes or rules govern the procedure to be followed.

B8.1

Any person may apply to make any child a ward of court except that a child who is subject to a care order may not be made a ward. A local authority may not use wardship and may only use the inherent jurisdiction with the leave of the court in exceptional circumstances.

CA 1989 section 100

B8.2

Once a child is made a ward of court, future decisions about the child must be made or approved by the court.

B8.3

The wardship court may make a wide variety of orders, on the principle that the ward's welfare is its paramount consideration. It cannot, however, make an order under the "inherent jurisdiction" which would have the same legal effect as a care or supervision order in favour of a local authority.

CA 1989 section 100

B9 Child abduction

The taking or detaining of a child under 16, so as to remove or keep the child from the lawful control of someone who has, or is entitled to have, lawful control of the child (i.e. has parental responsibility) is a criminal offence. The unmarried father of a child may have a specific defence in law. Removal of a child from the UK without appropriate consent may also be an offence.

Child Abduction Act 1984 sections 1 and 2

The Hague Convention on the Civil Aspects of International Child Abduction is incorporated into UK law by the Child Abduction and Custody Act 1985.

B10 Obligation to maintain children financially

Birth parents, with or without parental responsibility, and adoptive parents, are obliged to maintain their children, even if they are not having contact with them. Financial liability is ended only by the child being adopted by others. The granting of a special guardianship order does not end this liability. Most maintenance arrangements are by agreement or are governed by the Child Support Agency.

Child Support Act 1991 section 1

Where a child is looked after by a local authority (see Section E), it must maintain the child. With certain exceptions, the local authority must consider whether to seek a financial contribution from a parent or other person liable to contribute.

CA 1989 section 23(1) and (2), Schedule 2 paragraph 21

C

Local authority responsibilities to children and families

C1 The general duty of support for children in need

Local authorities are under a statutory duty to safeguard and promote the welfare of children in their area who are in need and, so far as is consistent with their welfare, to promote their upbringing by their families.

CA 1989 section 17

Child in need in Part III of the Children Act means a child who

a) 'is unlikely to achieve or maintain, or to have the opportunity of achieving or maintaining, a reasonable standard of health or development without the provision for him of services by a local authority or whose

b) health or development is likely to be significantly impaired, or further impaired, without the provision for him of such services or who

c) is disabled'.

CA 1989 section 17

C2 Provision of services

Local authorities have a duty to ensure the provision of certain services for children in need in their area. The range and level of services for an individual child are left to the local authority's discretion, but the services for children in need generally must include:

- day care for pre-school children;

- holiday and out-of-school care for school-age children;

- services for disabled children;

- schemes to reduce the need for care proceedings or criminal proceedings in respect of children; and

- advice, guidance and counselling.

In addition, local authorities are required to maintain registers of disabled children, and to publicise their services.

CA 1989 section 17 and Schedule 2 part 1

Local authorities are permitted to provide assistance in kind, accommodation or cash.

CA 1989 section 17(6) as amended by ACA 2002 and CYPA 2008

Before determining what (if any) services to provide for a particular child in need (including accommodation), a local authority shall, so far as is reasonably practical and consistent with the child's welfare:

(a) 'ascertain the child's wishes and feelings regarding the provision of those services: and

(b) give due consideration (having regard to the child's age and understanding) to such wishes and feelings as they have been able to ascertain'.

CA 1989 sections 17(4A) and 20(6) as amended by Children Act 2004 section 53(1) and (2)

Local authorities are also obliged to ensure the provision of services for people affected by adoption – see H13 and special guardianship (B7.5).

C3 Accommodation

Local authorities are required to provide accommodation for children in need who require it as a result of

- there being no person with parental responsibility for them;

- their being lost or abandoned;

- their carers being prevented (for whatever reason) from providing them with suitable accommodation or care.

They are also required to provide accommodation for 16- and 17-year-olds whose welfare is likely to be seriously prejudiced without it.

CA 1989 section 20

The local authority has discretion in extreme cases to accommodate a child with his/her parents where they might otherwise have to be separated.

CA 1989 section 17(6) as amended by ACA 2002 section 116(1)

C3.1

If the circumstances are not such as to require the local authority to provide accommodation, it may still do so if it considers that it would safeguard a child's welfare.

C3.2

The acceptance of accommodation is entirely voluntary and a local authority may not provide or continue to provide accommodation for a child under 16 against the wishes of the person or persons with parental responsibility who are willing and able to provide or arrange accommodation. If, however, a person is named in a child arrangements order as a person with whom a child should live or is a special guardian of the child and agrees to the provision of accommodation, the local authority may continue to provide it even if the parents with parental responsibility object. Where the child is 16 or 17, the agreement to accommodation must be the child's.

CA 1989 section 20(7)–(11) as amended by ACA 2002 section 139(1), (3) Schedule 3 paras 54 and 59

Child protection

D1 Duty to investigate

Local authorities have a statutory duty to investigate, as the lead agency, when allegations or suspicions of abuse are raised by other agencies or members of the public. Statutory guidance sets out the legal obligations for safeguarding and promoting the welfare of children for all key local people and bodies named under section 11(1) of the Children Act 2004, including health authorities and NHS trusts, police authorities and probation boards, youth offending teams, prison and secure training centre governors and persons providing services under section 114 of the Learning and Skills Act 2000.

When making a determination as to the action to be taken in respect of a child, a local authority shall, so far as is practicable and consistent with the child's welfare

(a) 'ascertain the child's wishes and feelings regarding the action to be taken

(b) give due consideration (having regard to the child's age and under-standing) to such wishes and feelings as they have been able to ascertain'.

CA 1989 section 47 as amended by Children Act 2004 section 53(3)
Statutory guidance to section 11 of the Children Act 2004

In any private family proceedings (for example, an application for a section 8 order or an adoption order), the court may direct the local authority to make enquiries to establish whether it should intervene to protect a child by, for example, applying for a care or supervision order. The court may not make a care or supervision order (except an interim order) unless an application is made by a local authority or the National Society for the Prevention of Cruelty to Children (NSPCC).

CA 1989 sections 31 and 37

D2 Emergency protection order

In some circumstances, where a child is suffering or is at risk of suffering significant harm, it is necessary as a matter of urgency to remove a child from home (or to prevent their removal from, for example, a foster home or hospital). It may be sufficient to commence care proceedings on notice to parents by applying for an interim care order, but an emergency protection order is available to allow rapid intervention to ensure the welfare of a child.

D2.1

The emergency protection order gives parental responsibility to the applicant, directs any person in a position to do so to produce the child, and authorises the applicant to remove the child to accommodation provided by the applicant and keep the child there, or prevent the child's removal from a hospital or other place.

CA 1989 section 44

D2.2

Anyone may apply for an emergency protection order but the court must be satisfied that there is reasonable cause to believe that the child is likely to suffer significant harm if not removed to accommodation provided by the applicant, or does not remain in the place in which the child is currently being accommodated, or that enquiries by a local authority or the NSPCC following suspicion of significant harm are being frustrated by an unreasonable denial of access to the child.

CA 1989 section 44(1)

D2.3

An emergency protection order may, if leave is given, be applied for without giving notice to the child or parents. The order can last for a maximum of eight days, but may be discharged earlier if an application is made to do so any time after 72 hours.

CA 1989 section 45

D2.4

If it is necessary to enter property without the permission of the owner, an application may be made for a warrant authorising a police officer to assist the applicant in exercising the powers under the emergency protection order, by force if necessary.

CA 1989 section 48(9)

D2.5

An emergency protection order may be extended once for a further period of up to seven days. Once it has expired there is no power to keep the child. An application must be made for a care order if it is felt that the child should remain in local authority care.

CA 1989 section 45(4)–(6)

D2.6

On making an emergency protection order the court may, if the legal criteria are met, attach an exclusion requirement so that an alleged abuser of the child can be removed or kept away from the child's home or the area around it. A power of arrest can be attached to the exclusion requirement.

CA 1989 section 44A

D3 Interim care and supervision orders

Since it is very unlikely that an application for a care or supervision order can be dealt with to final conclusion at the initial application hearing, the court can make an interim care or supervision order if it is satisfied that there are reasonable grounds for believing that the criteria for making a full order will be satisfied.

CA 1989 section 38

D3.1

An **interim care order** has the same legal effect as a care order, with the addition that the court may make orders (directions) with regard to medical examination or other assessment of the child.

CA 1989 sections 31(11) and 38(6) and (7)

D3.2

On making an interim care order, the court may attach an exclusion requirement so that an alleged abuser of the child can be removed or kept away from the child's home or the area around it. A power of arrest can be attached to the exclusion requirement.

CA 1989 section 38A

D4 Police protection

Police also have powers to protect children in emergencies. A police officer who has reasonable cause to believe a child would otherwise suffer significant harm may remove a child to suitable accommodation or prevent a child's removal from a place such as a hospital. The local authority, the child, and his or her parents must be informed as soon as possible, and a designated police officer must enquire into the circumstances. Police protection may only last for a maximum of 72 hours but the designated police officer may apply to the court for an emergency protection order.

CA 1989 section 46

D5 Child assessment orders

Where a local authority (or the NSPCC) has reasonable cause to believe that a child is suffering or is likely to suffer significant harm and they need an assessment of the child's health or development to enable them to ascertain this, they may apply to the court for a child assessment order if it is unlikely that the assessment will be made satisfactorily, or at all, without one. Any person who is in a position to do so must produce the child and comply with the directions in the order. The order will specify when the assessment is to begin and how long the order is to last (for a maximum of seven days), and is authority for the person(s) named in the order to carry out the assessment, subject to the right of a child of sufficient understanding to refuse to submit to an examination or assessment.

CA 1989 section 43

D5.1

If it is necessary for the assessment, the order may permit the child to be kept away from home for a period or periods specified in the order and, if it does so, the court may include directions as to contact between the child and other people.

D5.2

At least seven days' notice of an application for a child assessment order must be given to the child, his or her parents or carers, and certain other people closely involved with the child.

D5.3

The court may treat an application for a child assessment order as if it were an application for an emergency protection order and must make that order instead if it is satisfied that it ought to do so and that there are grounds for an emergency protection order.

CA 1989 section 43(3)

A child assessment order may not be applied for if a placement for adoption order has been made.

ACA 2002 section 29(3)(b)

D6 Care and supervision orders

These orders authorise intervention by a local authority in family life where a child is suffering or at risk of suffering significant harm.

D6.1

No care order can be made with respect to a young person who has reached 17, or 16 if they have married or entered into a civil partnership.

CA 1989 section 31(3)

A court may only make a care or supervision order if it is satisfied

a) that the child concerned is suffering, or is likely to suffer, significant harm, and

b) that the harm, or likelihood of harm, is attributable to

    (i) the care given to the child, or likely to be given to him if the order were not made, not being what it would be reasonable to expect a parent to give to him (or her); or

    (ii) the child's being beyond parental control.

D6.2

Even if the court is satisfied that this is so, it cannot make an order unless it considers that the order would be in the best interests of the child. The court cannot make a final care order unless the court has considered a section 31A care plan.

CA 1989 section 31(3A) as amended by ACA 2002 section 121(2)
CA 1989 section 1(5)

D6.3

The orders a court may make under section 31 are

- a **care order**, which gives parental responsibility for the child to the local authority, which then shares it with the birth parents and others with parental responsibility (including step-parents, guardians and special guardians). The local authority may determine the extent to which the parents and others with parental responsibility may continue to exercise it. The local authority may not, however, give consent to a child's placement for adoption or adoption, change the child's religion, or appoint a guardian. While the order is in force, no one may cause the child to be known by a new surname or permit the child to live outside the UK for more than one month without the leave of the court, or the consent of everyone who has parental responsibility.

CA 1989 section 33

- a **supervision order**, which places the child under the supervision of the local authority or, occasionally, a probation officer. A supervision order does not give parental responsibility to the local authority. The supervisor's duty is to 'advise, assist and befriend' the child and the court may attach certain requirements to the order for the child to comply with.

CA 1989 section 35

D6.4

Care proceedings are "family proceedings" under the Children Act 1989 and the court may make any section 8 order or a special guardianship order instead of a care order or supervision order.

CA 1989 sections 8 and 10 and 14A

D6.5

A care order lasts until the child becomes 18 unless it comes to an end earlier by:

● the child being adopted;

● the order being discharged by the court;

● the making of a child arrangements order specifying with whom the child should live;

● the making of a special guardianship order.

The making of a placement order suspends but does not discharge the care order.

CA 1989 sections 14 and 39 and ACA 2002 sections 21(1) and 46

D6.6

A supervision order lasts for one year or such shorter period as the court determines. It may be extended up to a maximum of three years, but cannot extend beyond the child's 18th birthday. It may be discharged on application and will be discharged by the making of:

● a care order;

● a placement order; or

● an adoption order; or

- a special guardianship order.

*CA 1989 section 91(3) sections 14 and 39 and
ACA 2002 sections 21(1), 29(2) and 46*

A supervision order may not be applied for if a child is subject to a placement for adoption order.

ACA 2002 section 29(3) (b)

Discharge of care order

D6.7

The child, the local authority, the parents, or other persons with parental responsibility may apply to the court to discharge a care order. Anyone entitled to do so, or who has obtained the court's leave, may apply for a child arrangements order, or special guardianship order, which discharges a care order.

A care order does not have legal effect if a placement order has been made, and therefore no application to discharge can be made during this time.

*CA 1989 section 39
ACA 2002 section 29(1)*

Discharge of supervision order

D6.8

The child, the supervisor or a person with parental responsibility may apply to discharge the supervision order. A supervision order is discharged by the making of a care order or placement order.

CA 1989 section 39 and ACA 2002 section 29(2)

D6.9 Legal advice and representation for parents in court proceedings

Birth parents with or without parental responsibility are automatically entitled to public funding to pay the costs of legal advice and representation in applications for care or supervision orders (and, in some situations, placement orders applied for within care proceedings – see Section H).

D6.10 Representing the child in care proceedings

In care order proceedings, the court will appoint a children's guardian, who is a qualified and experienced social worker independent of the local authority, from CAFCASS or a WFPO.

The duties of the children's guardian include investigating matters relating to the welfare of a child involved in the court proceeding, as set out in the court rules, and ensuring that the child's wishes and feelings are heard in court. The child will also usually be represented by a solicitor (whose costs are publicly funded). The child's solicitor represents the child's interests and wishes and is instructed by the children's guardian. However, if a child is deemed by his or her solicitor to be competent to instruct them directly, the solicitor must represent the child's rights, and their views, to the court, even if they differ from what the children's guardian recommends to be in the best interests of the child.

CA 1989 section 41

Children looked after by local authorities

E1 Powers and duties of local authorities

Children may be provided with care and accommodation by a local authority under several different provisions, or they may be subject to care orders or have been authorised to be placed for adoption. All such children are described as being "looked after" by the local authority.

Looked after children who are "in care" are those who are subject to a care order or interim care order under section 31 of the Children Act 1989.

Looked after children not "in care" include:

- children accommodated under section 20 CA 1989;

- children subject to emergency protection orders or in police protection;

- children on remand, or children who are the subject of some orders made by the youth (criminal) court;

- children who have been authorised to be placed for adoption by parental consent or a placement order;

- children freed for adoption under the Adoption Act 1976 (there will still be some freeing orders in force after these orders were abolished on 30 December 2005).

CA 1989 sections 20 and 21 and ACA 2002 sections 19 and 21

Once children are looked after, the local authority must provide accommodation and maintenance for them and safeguard their welfare in accordance with the Children Act 1989, and Regulations made under this Act and the Adoption and Children Act 2002.

E2 Principles to be followed

Welfare

The local authority has a duty to safeguard and promote the welfare of children whom it is looking after and to make such use of services available for children cared for by their own parents as appears reasonable, including promotion of the child's educational achievement.

CA 1989 section 22(3) and (3A) (amended by Children Act 2004 section 52)

Consultation

Before making any decision the local authority must, as far as is practicable, ascertain the wishes and feelings of the child, his or her parents or other people with parental responsibility, and any other person with a reasonable interest, and must give due regard to those wishes and feelings, having regard to the child's age and understanding, and the child's religious persuasion, racial origin, and cultural and linguistic background.

CA 1989 section 22(4) and (5)

"Authorised" children and consultation with parents

If a child has been authorised to be placed for adoption (see Section H), the duty to ascertain the wishes and feelings of parents or guardians under section 22(4) and (5) of the CA 1989 does not apply.

ACA 2002 section 53 and AAR 2005 Reg 45

E3 Care planning for looked after children

The local authority is required, in consultation with the child and parents, to prepare a care plan in respect of each child it is looking after, and care plans should be kept under review (see Section F).

A court cannot make a care order until it has considered a care plan submitted by the local authority.

CA 1989 section 31A

E3.1 Placement of looked after children

The local authority should, if practicable and consistent with the child's welfare, ensure that they are placed near home, and that siblings are accommodated together, and that, where a child is disabled, the accommodation is suitable to the child's particular needs.

CA 1989 section 22(c)(7) and (8)
CPPCR 2010

The Care Planning Regulations do not apply in respect of children authorised to be placed for adoption.

E3.2

The local authority should, if practicable and consistent with the child's welfare, make arrangements to enable the child to live with a parent or person with parental responsibility. If they cannot, they must give preference to a friend or relative who is also a foster carer.

E3.3

Where a local authority in England (but not in Wales) is considering adoption for a child, but is not authorised to place the child for adoption, they must consider placing the child with a relative or friend who is also a foster carer, or, if they consider that this is not the most appropriate placement, must consider placing the child with a foster carer who has been approved as a prospective adopter, in a fostering for adoption placement.

CA 1989 section 9A and 9B
CA 1989 section 22C(2)–(7)

E4 Foster care for looked after children

Children may be placed with foster carers, who may include the child's relatives.

E4.1

Before a child can be placed with any foster carers, they must have been approved by a local authority or a registered independent fostering service provider and the approval must be reviewed regularly.

- An agreement must be signed by the foster carers and the local authority in respect of each child placed.

- The child must be visited at specific intervals, which vary according to the length of time a child has been in the placement.

- The local authority must keep records of foster children and of visits to foster homes.

E4.2

When foster carers are approved, they and the local authority or fostering service provider must sign an agreement that includes the following:

- the support and training to be given to the foster carers;

- procedures for review of approval and the placement of children;

- the foster carer's agreement to care for any child placed as if he or she were a member of the foster carer's family;

- the foster carer's agreement to allow any child placed to be removed by the local authority;

- an agreement not to use corporal punishment; and

- confidentiality.

FSR 2011

E4.3 Independent fostering service providers (IFPs)

Looked after children may be placed by local authorities with foster carers recruited by IFPs, which are required to comply with the National Standards for Fostering Services, the Fostering Services Regulations 2002, and be registered and inspected by the Commission for Social Care Inspection.

An IFP is required to enter into formal agreements with the local authority referring children about the range of services provided to the children in foster placements, e.g. who supervises and reviews the placements.

FSR 2011

E4.4 Temporary approval of connected persons

In England only, a relative, friend or other person connected with a child may be approved as a temporary foster carer if the child's welfare requires immediate placement with that person. The connected person must have an assessment of suitability before the child is placed and must immediately begin a full assessment as a foster carer. Temporary approval may last for up to 16 weeks, and be extended for a period of eight weeks subject to certain conditions. If the connected person is not approved as a foster carer at the end of that period, the child must be removed from the placement.

CPPCRR 2010 Regs 24 and 25

E4.5 Temporary approval of prospective adopters

In England only, where a local authority proposes to make a fostering for adoption placement with a person who is approved as a prospective adopter but not as a foster carer, they may approve the adopter as a foster carer for a temporary period. There is no time limit on the period of temporary approval, which comes to an end on the occurrence of certain events.

CPPCRR 2010 Reg 25A

E5 Residential care of looked after children

Children may be placed in residential homes that are provided by the local authority or other organisations. All residential homes for children must be registered and inspected by OFSTED/CSSIW and must comply with National Minimum Standards for Children's Homes and The Children's Homes Regulations 2001 (England) and 2002 (Wales).

Children Act 1989 Guidance & Regulations Volume 5: Children's Homes (DfE 2013)

E6 Contact for looked after children

The local authority has a general duty to promote contact between children it is looking after and their parents, relatives, friends and other people connected with them, so far as is practicable and consistent with the child's welfare. The local authority has power to help with the cost of visits to or by a child in cases of hardship. The duty to promote contact does not apply if the child is authorised to be placed for adoption.

CA 1989 Schedule 2 paras 15 and 16
AAR 2005 Reg 45

E6.1

When a child is accommodated, the arrangements for contact should be agreed between the local authority, the parents and the child (if old enough) at the start of the placement and reviewed thereafter.

If contact arrangements cannot be agreed, the parents of a child in accommodation may apply to the court for a contact order under section 8 or remove the child from accommodation if they are entitled to do so.

E6.2 Contact and emergency protection orders

When a child is subject to an emergency protection order, the court may make directions as to the contact that is or is not allowed between the child and any named person. In the absence of a direction, the person who holds the emergency protection order must allow the child reasonable contact with parents, anyone with parental responsibility, the person with whom he or she was living when the order was made, and any person entitled to contact under a section 8 contact order.

CA 1989 section 44(6) and (13)

E6.3 Contact for children in care

When making a care order or interim care order, the court must consider the arrangements for contact between the child and parents and others, and may make an order with regard to contact, including an order giving permission for a local authority to refuse contact. Whilst a child is subject to a care order or interim care order, the local authority must allow the child reasonable contact with his or her parents or guardian and anyone previously providing care for him or her under a court order, until and unless an order to the contrary is made.

CA 1989 section 34(4) (5) and (11) and Schedule 2 para 15

E6.4 Orders for contact

A parent, or anybody with parental responsibility, or the local authority, or the child, or anyone with the court's permission, may apply to the court for an order defining the contact that is to take place.The court may also make a section 34 order even if no application has been made.

CA 1989 section 34(2) and (3)

E6.5 Refusal of contact

The local authority may apply to the court for an order under section 34(4) for permission to refuse contact between the child and a parent, guardian or previous carer. In an emergency, the local authority, to safeguard the child's welfare, may refuse contact for a maximum of seven days without a section 34(4) order, or in contravention of a section 34(3) order.

CA 1989 section 34(4) and (6)

E7 Secure accommodation

A child may not be placed in secure accommodation unless this is necessary because the child has a history of absconding and is likely to abscond and suffer significant harm, or because he or she is likely to injure him or herself or other people if kept in other accommodation. Different criteria apply to children who are required to be kept in secure accommodation because of criminal offending.

The permission of the Secretary of State is required before a child under 13 may be placed in secure accommodation.

CA 1989 section 25 and Children (Secure Accommodation) Regulations 1991
Children (Secure Accommodation) (Amendment) (Wales) Regulations 2013

Children cannot be placed in secure accommodation for more than 72 hours in any four weeks without a court order. The court will specify a maximum period for the use of secure accommodation (which cannot be more than three months initially, or six months on a further application) and the local authority must review the placement within one month, and thereafter at least every three months.

Children (Secure Accommodation) Regulations 1991

E8 Children leaving care or ceasing to be looked after

The local authority has statutory responsibilities and duties towards young people aged 16 and over who have been looked after, including preparing the young person for this change. Duties include advice, assistance and befriending, and assessing the young person's needs with a view to determining what advice, assistance and support would be appropriate and making a pathway plan, to be reviewed regularly.

CA 1989 Schedule 2, as inserted by Children (Leaving Care) Act 2000 and Children Leaving Care Regulations 2001 Reg 3 and Children (Leaving Care) (Wales) Regulations 2001 Reg 3

F

Reviews of looked after children

Local authorities have a statutory duty to review the case of each child they are looking after at regular intervals. The detailed requirements are set out in the Review Regulations.

Children authorised to be placed for adoption must also be reviewed – see Section H.

CA 1989 section 26
Review Regulations 2007 (Wales), and 2010 (England)

F1 The first review

The first review must take place within four weeks of the child first becoming looked after, and the next review no later than three months thereafter. Further reviews must take place at intervals of not more than six months.

Review Regulations

F2 Permanence planning

Adoption Statutory Guidance (2014) requires that the child's need for a permanent home should be addressed and a permanence plan made no later than the four-month review.

The plan made at this stage may include several options for permanence being explored at the same time – e.g. where appropriate, return home, kinship care, fostering or adoption – this is often known as "twin track" planning.

If and when adoption is identified as the preferred option for permanence at a review, the agency decision maker's decision on whether the child should be placed for adoption should be made within two months of that review.

However, this timetable can be departed from if it is not considered to be in the best interests of the child.

Adoption Guidance 2014 chapter 1 para 1.1

F3 Children who are looked after for short breaks

Children who are looked after on a regular basis for short periods each time (no more than four weeks in Wales or seven days in England) must have their cases reviewed, but each period of accommodation does not have to be treated as a separate episode for the purpose of reviews, or visiting requirements, provided the child stays in the same place each time.

Review Regs Reg 48 (England), Reg 12 (Wales)

F4 Independent Reviewing Officers

Local authorities looking after children must appoint independent reviewing officers (IROs) to ensure that children are reviewed according to regulations and to monitor the implementation of the care plans for the children, with the aim of minimising "drift" and challenging poor practice. The IRO should ensure that plans for looked after children are timely, effective and sensitive to needs, and should correct defects in implementation.

In between reviews, there is a statutory duty for the local authority to inform the IRO about a significant failure to implement decisions made as a result of a review, or significant changes in circumstances after the review that affect the plan for the child.

CA 1989 section 26 – as amended by ACA 2002 section 118
Review Regulations

F4.1 Problem-solving role for IROs

If problems in the implementation of care plans are identified, IROs have a duty to attempt to resolve them by negotiation with the local authority up to the highest level.

The IROs should also inform children of their rights to complaints and advocacy services and assist the child to obtain legal advice and take legal action and/or establish whether an appropriate adult is able and willing to bring proceedings on the child's behalf.

If all other methods of resolving a problem are unsuccessful, and where a child's human rights are considered to be in breach, an IRO should consider referral to CAFCASS or the Welsh equivalent so that legal proceedings can be considered to achieve the outcome sought by or on behalf of the child.

Possible legal action by CAFCASS includes further court proceedings, Human Rights Act applications or Judicial Review.

Review Regulations and Independent Reviewing Officers Handbook 2010

Representations, complaints and advocacy services for children

G1

Local authorities are required to establish a procedure for considering any representations, including complaints, made by:

- children looked after by them;
- children not looked after by them but in need;
- parents of such children;
- local authority foster carers; or
- other people with sufficient interest in the children.

Complaints can be made about services or accommodation provided, or refusal to provide accommodation, under Part III of the Children Act.

CA 1989 section 26(3)

The Representations and Complaints Procedure is not available to allow challenges to the local authority's decision to commence care or placement proceedings. These challenges should be made to the court.

The complaints procedure must be publicised and must comply with the Children Act 1989 Representations Procedure (England) Regulations 2006 and the Representations Procedure (Children) (Wales) Regulations 2005. A person independent of the local authority must be involved in the consideration of representations or complaints.

CA 1989 section 26(4) and (8)

G2 Advocacy services and representations procedure

Regulations impose a duty on local authorities to provide advocacy services for children wishing to make complaints under the Children Act 1989 representations procedure, and to make arrangements for the provision of assistance including by way of representation to care leavers and children who make or intend to make complaints.

CA 1989 sections 24D and 26(3)
Advocacy Services and Representations Procedure (Children) Amendment Regulations 2004, and The Advocacy Services and Representations Procedure (Children) (Wales) Regulations 2004

Adoption

H1 The welfare of the child is paramount

In reaching any decision about adoption, including placement for adoption, the welfare of the child throughout life is the paramount consideration for courts and adoption agencies. The Act also sets out a checklist of matters that must be taken into account, including consulting parents and guardians, ascertaining the child's wishes and feelings and giving due consideration to them (having regard to their age and understanding).

Courts and agencies must also bear in mind that any delay in coming to a decision is likely to prejudice the welfare of the child and must consider the whole range of powers available to them, under the CA 1989 and ACA 2002, and the court must not make any order unless it considers that making the order would be better for the child than not doing so.

ACA 2002 section 1

H2 The legal effect of an adoption order

An adoption order transfers parental responsibility for the child from birth parents and others who had parental responsibility, including the local authority, permanently and solely to the adopters. The child is deemed to be the child of the adopter or adopters as if he or she had been born to them in marriage. The child's name is usually changed to that of the adopters. The child's birth certificate is replaced by an adoption certificate showing the adopters to be the child's parents. Inheritance is from the adoptive family, not the birth family. A child who is not already a citizen of the UK acquires British citizenship if adopted in the UK by a citizen of the UK, or if adopted abroad under the Hague Convention by a British citizen.

H3 Prohibition of private placements

Private placements made in the UK (i.e. those not made by an adoption agency) are illegal except where the proposed adopter is a close relative of the child or the placement is made under a High Court order.

ACA 2002 section 92(3) and (4), section 144 (see H8 and A5 for definition of "relative") (as amended by the CPA 2004)

H4 Who can be adopted?

A child or young person who is to be adopted must not be married or have entered into a civil partnership, can be of any nationality and must be 18 or under. The application for the adoption order must be made before the young person's 18th birthday.

ACA 2002 section 47(8) and (9)

H5 Who can adopt?
H5.1 Age

An adoption order may only be granted to a person who is at least 21 years old, except that a birth parent adopting his or her birth child may be 18 or over. There is no legal upper age limit.

ACA 2002 sections 50 and 51

H5.2 Adoption by a couple

An adoption order may be granted to a couple whether or not they are married, or civil partners. The definition of a couple includes, as well as married and civil partnership couples, two people (whether of different sexes or the same sex) living together in an enduring family relationship, but excludes people who are related to each other as parent and child, or grandparent, sibling, aunt or uncle.

ACA 2002 section 50

H5.3 Adoption by one person

A sole adopter must be single, or if married or in a civil partnership, can adopt without his or her married or civil partner only in certain circumstances.

ACA 2002 section 51(2)

H5.4 Adoption by a step-parent

A step-parent (partner of a birth parent), whether or not they are married to or in a civil partnership with the birth parent, can apply on their own for an adoption order. (See Sections H12.1 and A6 Step-parents and parental responsibility.)

The birth parent need not adopt the child, and the adoption order does not change the legal position of the birth parent partner. However, the adoption order to the step-parent ends any parental responsibility held by the other birth parent.

ACA 2002 sections 51(1) and (2)

H5.5 Domicile or habitual residence

A single person or one of an applicant couple must be domiciled in the UK, Channel Islands or Isle of Man, or each applicant must have been habitually resident in any part of the British Islands for at least one year preceding their application for an adoption order.

ACA 2002 section 49(1-3)

H5.6 Eligibility to adopt from overseas

Eligibility to obtain an adoption order in England or Wales for a child from another country will also require compliance with the rules pertaining to that country (see H12 – Intercountry adoption).

H6 Adoptions arranged by adoption agencies

All adoption agencies – that is, local authorities and registered voluntary adoption agencies – are required to comply with the Regulations which govern, among other things, the referral of cases to adoption panels, the assessment and approval of proposed adopters and the supervision and review of adoption placements. Sections 18–35 ACA 2002 establish a framework for agency adoption placements.

ACA 2002 sections 18–35
AA Regulations 2005
SAR Regulations 2005
AFER Regulations 2005
Adoption Guidance 2014

Adoption is the choice made by some birth parents wishing to relinquish their children permanently to the care of others; it is also sometimes the choice made by local authorities for looked after children whose welfare requires permanent placement in another family.

H6.1 Authorising placement for adoption

If and when the local authority excludes other options for permanence as not in the child's best interests, and adoption is identified as the plan for permanence, the child may only be placed for adoption when the local authority is authorised to do so by a placement order, or the giving of section 19 consent by the child's parents or guardians.

ACA 2002 sections 18, 19(1) and 21(1) and AAR 2005 Reg 35(4)

A care order, or informal parental request to place a child over six weeks for adoption, is not authorisation.

H6.2 Parental consent to placement for adoption – section 19

For definition of "parent" or "guardian" in adoption law, see H8. A birth mother cannot give formal consent under section 19 to her child's placement for adoption until her child is six weeks old. (For placement for adoption of a child less than six weeks old, see H7.)

Parents and guardians are entitled to receive information and counselling from the adoption agency, including about the legal consequences of giving formal consent.

They are also entitled to an explanation of the legal consequences from the CAFCASS officer or WFPO, who is independent of the adoption agency and appointed to ensure that consent is given with full understanding and unconditionally, and to witness the signature of the parents or guardians on the consent form.

ACA 2002 sections 18(1) and 19
AAR 2005 Reg 20
FPR 2010 Rule 14:10

The consent can be specific to placement with particular adopters, or for placement with any adopters chosen by the agency. Consent to placement can be withdrawn in writing to the adoption agency at any time before the adoption order is applied for.

ACA 2002 section 19(1)

Parents or guardians living abroad

Where the parents or guardians are outside England and Wales, their consent should be witnessed by a person authorised for this purpose. A CAFCASS officer is not appointed in respect of checking or witnessing their consent

FPR 2010 Rule 14:10

Advance consent to the making of an adoption order – section 20

At the time of giving section 19 consent, or subsequently, formal consent may also be given by parents and guardians to the making of an adoption order in favour of adopters chosen by the agency or adopters identified in the consent. At the same time, the parent or guardian may also give written notice that they do not wish to be notified of the subsequent application for an adoption order. If this notice is not given, parents and guardians must be notified by the court of the application for an adoption order.

ACA section 20(1) and (2)

Section 20 consent may be withdrawn by written notice to the adoption agency at any time before the adoption order is applied for.

ACA 2002 section 20(3)

H6.3 Placement orders

A placement order is a court order which entitles a local authority to place a child for adoption with any adopter(s) chosen by the authority.

A placement order may only be made if the court is satisfied that:

- the child is already subject to a care order under the Children Act 1989; or
- the child is suffering or at risk of suffering significant harm, attributable to the standard of parental care; or
- the child has no parent or guardian;

and

- each parent or guardian consents to the placement; or
- the court is satisfied that the consent should be dispensed with (see H8.3 for dispensation of consent).

ACA 2002 section 21

A placement order lasts until the child is adopted, or reaches the age of 18, or marries or enters into a civil partnership, unless it is revoked (see below).

Obligation to apply for a placement order

A local authority is obliged to apply for a placement order if it considers that the child should be placed for adoption but does not have parental consent to placement, and that the grounds for a placement order can be established, or if it is engaged in an application for a care order.

ACA 2002 section 22

Revocation of placement orders

An application for revocation of a placement order can be made at any time by a child or the local authority as of right.

Other people (including parents and guardians) can only apply if the court has given leave and the child has not been placed for adoption. The court may only give leave if there has been a change of circumstances since the placement order was made.

ACA 2002 section 24

H6.4 Legal consequences of authorisation to place

The most significant consequences of authorisation to place are the following.

- The agency acquires parental responsibility for the child, shared with the birth parents and the prospective adopters once the child is placed. However, the agency may restrict the exercise of parental responsibility of birth parents and/or prospective adopters. The child cannot be known by a new surname or removed from the UK (for more than one month) except with the written consent of each parent or guardian or the leave of the court.

- There are restrictions on the parents' ability to remove the child from placement.

- There are limits on applications or orders under the Children Act 1989.

- Contact orders under the Children Act 1989 no longer have effect and a local authority is not obliged to promote contact with parents.

- The parent or guardian will not be able to oppose the making of an adoption order without the leave of the court.

ACA 2002 sections 25, 26, 28–34
AAR 2005 Reg 45

On the making of a placement order, any section 8 order or supervision order under the Children Act 1989 is brought to an end. The parental responsibility of any special guardian is subject to any restriction imposed by the local authority, but is not brought to an end. A care order is suspended, but will be effective again if the placement order is revoked.

A birth father acquiring parental responsibility after the mother has consented and the child has been placed for adoption, is deemed to have given section 19 consent too.

ACA 2002 section 52(9) (a)

H7 Placement for adoption of a child under six weeks old

An agency may place a child under six weeks of age if the parents agree to this in writing with the adoption agency.

ACA 2002 section 18
AAR 2005 Reg 35(4)

The legal consequences

If the parents or guardians change their minds, their child must be returned by the agency within seven days, unless the local authority applies for a placement order. The issuing of an application for a placement order exempts the local authority from the duty to return the child to parents or guardians until the application is determined by the court.

ACA 2002 section 31(3)

Contact is at the discretion of the local authority, or section 26 contact orders can be made.

ACA 2002 section 26(1)

Prospective adopters and the local authority do not have parental responsibility.

ACA 2002 section 25(3)

When the child reaches six weeks of age, the agency will need to arrange for formal parental consent under section 19 or, if that is not possible, consider applying for a placement order.

H8 Consent and dispensing with consent

Adoption orders cannot be made unless:

- each parent or guardian consents to the making of the order; or
- consent to placement for adoption has previously been given under section 19 ACA 2002 and has not been withdrawn; or
- the child is subject to a placement order; or
- the court dispenses with consent.

H8.1 The meaning of parent or guardian in adoption law

"Parent" means each birth parent with parental responsibility for the child. "Guardian" means a legally appointed guardian (see A3) or a special guardian (see B7), but it does not include a person named in a child arrangements order, or a step-parent who has acquired parental responsibility by agreement or order.

ACA 2002 sections 52(6) and 144

H8.2 Birth fathers without parental responsibility

A birth father without parental responsibility is not automatically a party to court proceedings for placement and adoption orders, and he is not entitled to give, withhold or withdraw his consent to his child being placed for adoption, or to seek the court's leave to oppose the making of an adoption order.

However, in compliance with Articles 6 and 8 of the European Convention on Human Rights, courts are likely to be sympathetic to an application by a birth father without parental responsibility to be made a party to placement order or to adoption proceedings.

Where a father does not have parental responsibility and his identity is known to the adoption agency, and where the agency is satisfied that it is appropriate to do so, it must consult, counsel and advise him about his child being placed for adoption, and ascertain if he is intending to acquire parental responsibility or apply for a residence or contact order.

Directions can be sought by the agency from the court about notifying the father of the intention to place his child for adoption. If there are no current court proceedings, the application for directions should be made to the High Court.

AA Regs 2005 Reg 14(4)
FPR 2010 Rule 14:21
Adoption Guidance 2014

H8.3 Dispensing with parental consent to the making of an adoption order or a placement order

The court may dispense with the consent of a parent or guardian to the making of an adoption order or a placement order, on the grounds that

- the parent cannot be found;

- the parent is incapable of consenting; or

- the welfare of the child requires their consent to be dispensed with.

ACA 2002 section 52(1)

If a parent is expected to consent, the court will appoint a CAFCASS officer or a WFPO to witness their consent to an adoption or placement order.

H9 The court procedure

Adoption and placement order applications may be heard by any level of the Family Court. The public are excluded from all adoption court hearings.

Adoption and placement proceedings at every level of court are governed by the Family Procedure Rules 2010.

The procedure varies according to whether or not the child has been authorised to be placed for adoption, and whether or not the parents have consented to placement, a placement order has been made, or parents and guardians have been given leave to oppose the making of the adoption order.

H9.1 Children as parties to proceedings

Children are always parties to applications for placement orders and a children's guardian will be appointed by the court to safeguard the welfare of the child and appoint a solicitor for the child.

In adoption order applications the child will only be made a party in the circumstances set out in the court rules.

A court considering an application for an adoption order or section 84 order may ask a CAFCASS officer or WFPO to prepare a welfare report on the child. The writer of such a report is referred to in the rules as "children and family reporter" (the children and family reporter is a distinct role referred to in the court rules, although this person will be a CAFCASS officer or WFPO).

The duties of the children's guardian, the child's solicitor and the children and family reporter are set out in the court rules.

FPR 2010 Part 14

H9.2 The confidentiality of applicant adopters

If the identity of the applicants for an adoption order or section 84 order are not to be disclosed to the birth parents or guardians, the applicants will be given a serial number by the court, which will appear on all the papers instead of their names and addresses.

FPR 2010 Rule 14:2

H9.3 The confidentiality of court reports

The court will direct if and when confidential reports are disclosed to parties in adoption proceedings, including whether any information in the reports should be deleted before disclosure – e.g. to protect identities – and may direct that reports should not be disclosed.

FPR 2010 Rule 14:13

H9.4 Alternative court orders

Adoption order and placement order applications are "family proceedings", and the court can make Children Act 1989 or other Adoption and Children Act 2002 orders as well as, or instead of, these orders, whether or not an application has been made for them. It could, for example, refuse an adoption order but make a residence order or special guardianship order, or make a post-adoption contact order with the adoption order.

CA 1989 sections 8(3) & (4) and 10(1)
ACA 2002 section 1(6) and section 51A (inserted by the CFA 2014 section 9)

H10 Contact and adoption

H10.1 Agency adoption placements

Where children have been authorised to be placed for adoption, or placed for adoption by an agency (including those under six weeks of age), contact is at the discretion of the local authority – there is no duty to promote contact.

The child, the local authority, parents, guardians, relatives, holders of a previous contact or residence order, and those who had care of the child by a High Court order, can apply under section 26 for a contact order.

When the court makes a placement order, it must consider actual or proposed contact arrangements, and the views of the parties, and may make a contact order even if there has been no application for one.

ACA 2002 section 26(1) and section 144 for definition of "relative"

Others, including the child's prospective adopters, can apply for section 26 contact orders with the leave of the court.

ACA 2002 section 26(3) (f)

H10.2 Contact after adoption

It is not uncommon for an arrangement to be made for some form of continuing contact (often indirect, for example, by means of letters or cards) to continue after adoption between the child and members of his or her birth family.

Before making an adoption order, the court has a duty to consider whether there should be arrangements for contact (orders or undertakings) and hear the views of all the parties. There is no "presumption" of contact. Section 51A contact orders can be made with adoption orders on application by parents and guardians, or others with leave of the court, or of the court's own initiative.

ACA 2002 sections 1(6) and 46(6) and section 51A

Birth family members or others seeking a section 51A contact order after an adoption order has been granted, must first obtain leave of the court to apply.
ACA 2002 section 51A

H11 Non agency adoptions

H11.1 Step-parent adoption

The step-parent is a person who is not the child's birth parent, but is the partner of one of the child's birth parents.

A step-parent, if at least 21, can apply to adopt the child without the birth parent having to adopt too. The adoption order to the step-parent does not change the legal position of the birth parent partner, but ends any parental responsibility of the other birth parent.

Step-parents may apply for the adoption order when the child has lived with them for at least six months, and must give notice to the local authority for the area in which they have their home of their intention to apply for an adoption order, at least three months *before* the application can be started.

The local authority must investigate and provide a report to the court covering the matters detailed in the court rules.

ACA 2002 sections 42, 44 and 51
FPR 2010 Rule 14:11 and Practice Direction 14B

H11.2 Applications to adopt by relatives and private foster carers

Where the child has not been placed by an adoption agency, and the child's relatives or private foster carers are the adoptive applicants, they cannot apply for the adoption order until the child has lived with them for no less than three years (whether continuous or not) in the preceding five years, unless the court gives leave for an earlier application.

The applicants must give notice to the local authority in which they have their home of their intention to apply for an adoption order at least three months before the adoption order is applied for.

The local authority must investigate and provide a report to the court covering the matters detailed in the court rules.

ACA 2002 sections 42(5) and 44
FPR 2010 Rule 14:11 and PD 14B, Annex A

H11.3 Adoption by local authority foster carers

Normally the local authority would be expected to consider whether to assess foster carers with a view to approving them as agency adopters, but they can apply to adopt the child placed with them for fostering without that approval or the permission of the local authority or the court, when the child has lived with them continuously during the 12 months before the application, or earlier if the court gives leave. The foster carers must give three months' notice of their intention to apply for an adoption order to the local authority where they live before making the application.

The local authority must investigate and report to the court covering the matters detailed in the court rules.

ACA 2002 sections 42(4) and 44
FPR 2010 Rule 14:11 and PD 14, Annex A

H11.4 Application following an unlawful private placement

Since private placements, except with relatives or the leave of the High Court, are unlawful (see H3), any application that follows such a placement must be made to the High Court, which may, in the interests of the child's welfare, authorise the making of the order despite the illegality.

H12 Intercountry adoption

"Intercountry adoption" is a general term referring to the adoption of a child resident abroad by adopters resident in the United Kingdom; it may also refer to the adoption of a child resident in the United Kingdom by adopters resident overseas. The UK's ratification of the 1993 Hague Convention on Protection of Children and Co-operation in respect of Intercountry Adoption means that the UK is part of an international system of collaboration that aims to prevent the abduction of, sale of, or trafficking in children.

H12.1 Adoption of children from abroad in the UK

UK residents may adopt children from overseas subject to compliance with regulations. It is a criminal offence for anyone habitually resident in the British Islands to bring a child into the UK for adoption unless they meet the requirements of the regulations. For example:

- they must have been assessed and approved by a local authority or registered voluntary adoption agency in the UK, in accordance with Regulations;

- the approval must have been endorsed by the Secretary of State;

- the adopters(s) must inform their local authority within 14 days of the child's arrival into the UK of their intention to apply for an adoption order or intention not to continue to give a home to the child.

ACA 2002 Section 83
AFER 2005

H12.2 Removal of a child for the purposes of adoption from the UK

It is a criminal offence to remove a child from the UK, who is habitually resident here, for the purposes of adoption.

There must be compliance with regulations, and the prospective adopters must have obtained a section 84 order giving them parental responsibility for the child. The child must have been living with the prospective adopters for at least 10 weeks before an application can be made.

ACA 2002 sections 84 and 85
Adoption (Intercountry Aspects) Act 1999
The Adoptions with a Foreign Element Regulations 2005

H13 Adoption support

Local authorities are obliged to provide, or arrange the provision of, a range of prescribed adoption support services. Adopted children and adults, prospective and actual adopters, birth parents and, in so far as the regulations prescribe, other individuals, are entitled to an assessment of needs for adoption support in so far as the support service concerned is required by the Regulations to be made available to that category of person. Adoption support includes the provision of financial support, which may be made as a series of payments or in one or more lump sum. The provision of financial support will usually be subject to a means test, except in the circumstances prescribed in the regulations.

ACA 2002 sections 2–4 and 8
ASR 2005

H14 Birth records and contact between adult adopted people and birth relatives

H14.1 Access to birth records

On reaching the age of 18, adopted people have a right to obtain a copy of their original birth certificate. If the adoption order was made before 12 November 1975, they must receive counselling before the information will be given to them. People adopted after that date may have the information when they reach 18 and counselling is optional. If they were adopted before

30 December 2005, the application for this information is made direct to the Registrar General. If they were adopted on or after 30 December 2005, disclosure by the Registrar General will be made via the "appropriate" adoption agency, that is, the agency that arranged the adoption or the local authority that reported to court in a non-agency adoption, unless the High Court orders that it is not to be disclosed.

ACA 2002 section 79 and section 60 (2)

H14.2 Disclosure of information to an adopted adult about his/her adoption

Regulations prescribe the information an adoption agency must keep about a person's adoption – known as "section 56 information". Disclosure of some "protected" information is only permitted in circumstances set out in sections 56–65 of ACA 2002. Protected information means information that identifies an individual other than the person seeking the information.

An adopted adult also has the right to a copy of court documents relating to his/her adoption, subject to the deletion of protected information.

For people adopted before 30 December 2005, the preservation of confidentiality and the disclosure of adoption records is governed by the Adoption Agencies Regulations 1983.

FPR 2010 Rule 14:18 and PD 14F
The Disclosure of Adoption Information (Post-Commencement Adoptions)
Regulations 2005 – adoptions after 30 December 2005
The Adoption Agencies Regulations 1983 – adoptions before 30 December
2005

H14.3 Adoption Contact Register

Adopted adults and birth relatives can record their views about contact with each other on this register. The Registrar General maintains the Adoption Contact Register in two parts, one containing the names and addresses of adopted people and the other those of birth relatives. The register is not open to the general public. An application form must be completed and a fee paid for registration. If a match occurs between the two parts of the Register, an adopted person who registered a desire for contact is notified of the name and address of the relative.

ACA 2002 sections 80 and 81
The Adopted Children and Adoption Contact Registers Regulations 2005

Further reading

Government publications and guidance

- Volume 1 – Children Act 1989: Court Orders (DfE, April 2014)

- Volume 2 – Children Act 1989: Care Planning, Placement and Case Review (DfE, 2010, updated July 2014)

- Volume 3 – Children Act 1989: Transition to Adulthood for Care Leavers (DfE, 2010, updated October 2014)

- Volume 4 – Children Act 1989: Fostering Services (DfE, 2011)

- Volume 5 – Children Act 1989: Children's Homes (DfE, 2013)

This Guidance, first published in 1992 and periodically updated, is no longer available in book form and is now published and updated online only at https://www.gov.uk/.

Other books

Allen N (2007) *Making Sense of the New Adoption Law* (2nd edition), Lyme Regis: Russell House Publishing

A guide for non-lawyers, which is also useful to lawyers. Sets out the background to and the reasons for adoption law being reformed and the main implications of the Adoption and Children Act 2002.

Allen N (2005) *Making Sense of the Children Act 1989* (4th edition), Chichester: John Wiley and Sons Ltd

A guide for non-lawyers, which is also useful to lawyers. The 2005 edition includes amendments to the Children Act 1989 made by the Adoption and Children Act 2002 and the Children Act 2004.

Ball C (2005) *Child Care Law: Social work law file* (6th edition), Norwich: University of East Anglia

Hershman D and McFarlane A (2014) *Children Act Handbook 2014/5*, Bristol: Jordan Publishing

This handbook is updated annually. The 2014/5 edition includes amendments to the Children Act 1989 and to the Adoption and Children Act 2002 made by the Children & Families Act 2014.

Smith F and Stewart R with Conroy Harris A (2013) *Adoption Now*, London: BAAF

A third edition of an accessible and user-friendly pocket book for non-lawyers incorporates the Adoption and Children Act 2002 and other legislation relevant to adoption.

Smith F and Brann C with Conroy Harris A (2011) *Fostering Now*, London: BAAF

A second edition of this accessible user-friendly and user-friendly pocket book for non-lawyers on legislation relevant to fostering in England and Wales.

Reference works

Hershman D and McFarlane A, *Children Law and Practice*, Family Law.

This is a loose-leaf volume which is regularly updated. Also available on line or by CD-ROM.

Journal

Adoption & Fostering, the quarterly journal published by BAAF, contains new developments in child care practice, law and research. Also includes Legal Notes from around the UK.